The Evening Light

THE EVENING LIGHT

poems by

Floyd Skloot

Story Line Press
Ashland, Oregon

Published by Story Line Press, Three Oaks Farm, PO Box 1240, Ashland,
OR 97520-0055.

This publication was made possible thanks in part to the generous support of
the Nicholas Roerich Museum, the Andrew W. Mellon Foundation, The
Collins Foundation, the Rose E. Tucker Charitable Trust, the Oregon Arts
Commission, and our individual contributors.

Book design by Lysa McDowell
Oil painting, "On the Edge but Taking No Chances," by Kenneth Grant

Library of Congress Cataloging-in-Publication Data

Skloot, Floyd.
    The evening light : poems / by Floyd Skloot.
        p.   cm.
    ISBN 1-58654-000-9
    I. Title

PS3569.K577 E94 2001
811'.54—dc21   00-047102

Acknowledgements

Grateful acknowledgement is made to the following magazines, where some of these poems first appeared:

America, The Atlantic Monthly, The Bridge, Carolina Quarterly, Centennial Review, Chelsea, Clackamas Literary Review, Crazyhorse, Cyphers (Ireland), The Honest Ulsterman (N. Ireland), The Hudson Review, Image, InCognito (Ireland), JAMA: The Journal of the American Medical Association, Marlboro Review, Michigan Quarterly Review, The New Criterion, North American Review, Northwest Review, Notre Dame Review, Poetry, Poetry Daily, Poetry Ireland Review, Poetry New Zealand, Poetry Northwest, Prairie Schooner, Prism International (Canada), Quarterly West, Salmagundi, The Salt Journal, The Sewanee Review, Shenandoah, Silverfish Review, The Southern Review, Southern Poetry Review, Tracks (Ireland) and *Virginia Quarterly Review.*

"Daybreak" appeared in *The Atlantic Monthly*, April 1995.
"Sourwood Nocturne" appeared in *The Hudson Review*, Winter 1995.
"Bittersweet Nightshade" and "Glinka Dancing" appeared in *The Hudson Review*, Summer 1996.
"Frogs Returning Moon" and "Hop Fields in Winter" appeared in *The Hudson Review*, Spring 1997.
"Toomey's Diner" appeared in *The Hudson Review*, Autumn 1998.
"Self-Portrait with 1911 NY Yankees Cap" appeared in *Michigan Quarterly Review*, Summer 1998.
"Kokoschka in Love, 1914" appeared in *The New Criterion*, June 1996.
"Oncogene" appeared in *Salmagundi*, Summer 1999.
"Memory Harbor," "Seduction," and "Terminal" appeared in *The Sewanee Review*, Summer 1999.
"Manet in Late Summer" appeared in *Shenandoah*, Summer 1997.
"Autumn Equinox" appeared in *The Southern Review*, Spring 1998.
"A Change of Weather" appeared in *Virginia Quarterly Review*, Winter 2000.

I would like to thank the Villa Montalvo (Saratoga, CA) and the Heinrich Böll Foundation (Achill Island, Ireland) for residencies during the time when these poems were written. I am also grateful to the Oregon Arts Commission for a 1993 Individual Artist Fellowship and to Oregon Literary Arts, Inc., for the 1996 William Stafford Fellowship in Poetry.

For Thomas Kinsella

The waves, arguing among themselves
along the slope of shore, are alive,
hurrying in disorder between two stillnesses:

—from "High Tide: Amagansett,"
by Thomas Kinsella

CONTENTS

IV: Pure Gift

V: Daybreak

The Evening Light

I

AN INNER WIND

ARGENTEUIL, 1874

As summer sun stipples the garden grass,
Monet is watering his roses. Camille sits
in the noon light, chin on hand, white dress
a pillow for young Jean who no longer fits
across her lap. Missing the city, she
is ready to pack right now if only Claude
could tear himself away. But she knows he
wants to spend time painting with Edouard,
and Jean, half-asleep, is already talking about
having a picnic tomorrow. It is always
like this. Now Claude has brought his paints out
to sit beside Edouard and work till day's
end. At least he is turned away from her.

She sees what will happen even before
Pierre arrives. There is no wind to stir
the air, no cloud to change the light; what more
could they hope for? These are men who would paint
their wives on death-beds if the light were right.
Camille smiles and shifts Jean so that his weight
is off her thigh. Oh, they will eat fish tonight,
a red mullet or, better still, fresh eel,
only in her dreams. Perhaps they should
eat this hen and cock clucking at their heels.

After the last Salon, of course the men would
need something like this, a slow summer to
paint their hearts out, a blossoming of sheer
joy together. So there is nothing to do
but hold still in the heat and be here
with all one's heart—perhaps a quick flutter

of the fan to keep Jean calm and herself
fresh—as time slows and the men, in utter
concentration, begin to lose themselves

in the closed circle of their art and Manet
paints the Monets in their garden as Monet
paints a grinning Manet painting the Monets
in their garden and Renoir paints the Monets
in their garden in the summer in Argenteuil.

GLINKA DANCING

"My feet were all right,
but I couldn't manage the castanets."
—Mikhail Glinka, 1845

In the olive and wine-scented
light of a Seville summer night,
the Father of Russian Music
glowed garnet as he stomped
triple time through his first
Zapateado. This was better
than the stylized Seguidilla
he mastered in the smoky dark
of Madrid. It was closer to
his soul than the Fandango
with its hardwood and cord
castanets, or the Malaguena—
voluptuous as that gypsy woman
by the bar all draped in hemp
and jute, smiling at him now
in the mirror. What he loved
was the solo speed and harsh
mark his heels made on the weak
beat. He could feel the snap
and citrus color of the melody
searing his marrow. A dance
like fire and he needed fire.
In St. Petersburg they wanted
cool quadrilles, an evening
of fantasies on chic themes.
Here a man twisted and squirmed
in the arms of dark-eyed song.
Here a man courting wonder found
himself consumed by its flames.

KOKOSCHKA IN LOVE, 1914

It does not matter how a mountain found
its way into these waves. Perhaps the wind,
perhaps the war. He turns in predawn light
to find Alma's pale arms held as though bound

to the bedposts. Her eyes are giving back
their horde of pure darkness as though the night
were hers for good. He knows those eyes will rend
his flesh unless he paints them closed, the black

buried in swirling seas along with blood
and the morning's first full blue as the ship
their bare bed has become shatters. The lip
of the whirlpool will be gushing with gold

flecks of foam and silver will mark the clouds.
It is the tempest and she is the bride
of the wind fitted now against his side.
He will do it right if he can just hold

himself together long enough, if he
can disentangle himself before she
feels his absence or a chill in the air,
if he can leave her there without a sound.

DONIZETTI IN A COMA, BERGAMO, 1848

Donizetti told us music and home were
always the same. He could not forget
the clop of horse and carriage around
the Piazza Vecchia, or that he composed
his first operas to the sound of art
students chattering as they ran down
from the Carrara. Bergamask valleys
at dusk flared with birdsong and autumn
storms keening through the ancient trees.
From the open window of his room he loved
to hear the curfew bell's final note linger
on through frozen Alpine nights. So this
is where we brought him in his final sleep.

Five years ago, Donizetti told us Vienna
would be a place to rest. But all through June
he burned with fevers, his letters blotted
with what we took to be sweat. Back in Paris,
exhausted by an hour's work, he knew before
anyone that all the laughter was gone.
In the old days he would flit from Naples
to Milan to Venice to Bologna with no thought
of rest. A new opera every three months,
Masses and motets, quick psalms, string quartets.

But in Vienna, faint wisps of melody drifted
away like high clouds, shapeless and lost
as though spirited off by an inner wind.
He lay in bed till early afternoon.
He dreamed there were violet and saffron
silences bursting like catherine wheels
from his most elaborate cadenzas and woke
certain he had slit his own throat with threads
of a cello bow. He spoke in a trilling whisper
with his stillborn daughter, dead six years.

Soon he seemed to be moving as though air
would liquify at the very touch of his body.
Tea, a dog barking, or evening shadows
filled him with rages we dreaded to see.

Friends in Paris told us he would stare
into the Seine for hours, hair drenched by rain.
Books fell from his hands, tears from his eyes.
They blamed old griefs, his beloved wife Virginia
lost to cholera or childbirth, his failure
to attend his father's funeral, the sneers
of Berlioz. When Bellini vanished at thirty-four,
Donizetti never showed his anguish. It was all
those years of overwork, they said, crisscrossing
the continent for commissions. It was enemies
in Italy, that French alto ruining *Dom Sebastien*
on opening night. They watched him thin, fade.

Something strange had turned the great composer
of mad scenes mad himself. He told us he longed
to write an aria for the twenty voices in his head
at once, the way he had before in the sextet
from *Lucia di Lammermoor*. He said there would be
bel canto songs no one would ever forget,
duets crisp as duels, a music of sheer delirium
for coloratura soprano and mourning dove.

By the time Donizetti fled to Vienna again,
nothing could stir him to music, speech,
or the slightest gesture. We brought him
home to Bergamo, across the Po River Plain,
talking, singing, keeping his music alive.
Although his eyes remained shut, we placed
his stretcher for an hour under the dome
of the Colleoni Chapel, letting him be
among Tiepolo's frescoes one more time.
Then we carried him to this bed, to sleep
without waking in the place of his birth.

MANET IN LATE SUMMER

"The exquisite creations of these last months, when Manet was too exhausted to finish anything more demanding, were a series of paintings of flowers."
—Otto Friedrich, *Olympia: Paris in the Age of Manet*

With his eyes closed
the pain is cobalt
blue flaring to brilliant
orange whenever he is
touched. There are no
black edges and no shadows
to it, only this thick
burst of purest color
in a field spread sap
green to the horizon.

All week he has tried
to paint a young woman
on horseback, a bugler,
an Amazon, anything other
than flowers. Sunk to
the chest in warm water,
he nibbles a loaf of rye
bread tainted with ergot
and swears if he could rise
tonight he would slash
his last canvases to rags
with a palette knife.

As his movements shrink
the world grows too great.
All he knows must now be
contained in two clusters
of white lilacs, the cut
flowers flaring like hope

where they rest on black
cloth. His bath has cooled.
Across the room a vase
of pinks and clematis
catches the fading light.

SEURAT ON THE VERNAL EQUINOX, 1891

Georges Seurat died of diphtheria in Paris,
March 29, 1891. He was 31.

In the Pointillist painting of Georges Seurat
the precise placement of dots of pure color
forces a viewer's eyes to mix them much as
paint on a palette, thereby demonstrating

art's truly mutual nature. Surrounded
by paint pots, Seurat stands too close to his huge
canvas to see the effect he seeks, but that
does not matter. In fact, it is the essence

of what he has been trying to show! He holds
a half-dozen brushes between his knuckles
or gripped in his teeth, head teeming with theory.
The way light truly is, the way distance works

on a wave, the way the mind lies to the eyes—
if he can only get it right, there will be
a science of art, perception exactly
re-enacted in all its perfect pleasure.

But Seurat is not well. He would like to tell
Signac how close he is to the exquisite
balance at last. He would like to see the look
on Pissarro's face as he is overcome

by amazement. He would like for his mother
to know his child now; she should meet the woman
he has loved and hidden away. He would like
to rest, swallow without pain, breathe with the old

ease. He spreads his fingers to let the brushes
clatter to their rack, plucks one from his mouth, steps
forward. Yellow ocher for the earth. Next comes
a field of green. He thought there would be more time.

VAN GOGH AND TOULOUSE-LAUTREC ON THE WAY TO PERE TANGUY'S

From behind they look like father and son
hurrying down a wintry Paris street.

The one on the right speeds up as the one
on the left doffs his homburg, stops to greet
all the women, then shambles to rejoin
his lanky partner who casts suspicious
glances left and right. Henri takes a coin
from his pocket; Vincent hurls a vicious
look at the beggar reaching out for it.

He believes the poor need a different kind
of help, something to arouse the spirit.
It has not been long since he tried to find
the light inside a pauper's home himself.

He rubs a hand over the red stubble
of his beard and hair, singing to himself
a crude song he recalls from the rubble
of last night at the swanky cabaret
Henri favors. When the little man sleeps
is anyone's guess. Vincent wants to say
come along, wants to ask why Henri keeps
wasting time if he was in such a rush
to get there. They both need paints and Vincent
hopes old Tanguy will throw in a new brush
or two, and canvas, perhaps some solvent.

After all, Tanguy has seven Van Gogh's
stashed here and there. He would be a damn fool
to cut Vincent off now. Everyone knows
that though Tanguy is soft, he is no fool.

Hissing through his teeth, Vincent turns to see
a flash of sunlight off Henri's pince-nez.
Such a flabby face. He can see Henri's
bulging eyes even from this far away.

Poor man. Then Vincent notices his friend
has burst into crimson and yellow flame!
Nothing he can do. This must be the end
of Paris, a message from God. The same
thing happened outside Eindhoven a year
ago, friends erupting in fire that lit
a broad stand of cypresses. It was clear
to him then and he made the requisite
move in three days. Still, he will need supplies
if he is to capture what he has seen:

Out of fire, a dwarf come stumbling with cries
of joy on his moist lips, with blue and green
streaks weighing down his cheeks. Good Lord, the man
is odd looking. Suddenly Vincent hears
what this demon is shouting and he can
hardly believe it. Devil! Those are tears,
fading as he nears, and that is laughter
coming from his lips as he gasps *you are
looking wild, my friend. Is someone after
you?* and takes Vincent's arm. It is not fair,
it is the same thing all over again.

He mutters in English, then French, then Dutch,
thinking he must be near flowers, not men,
he must have peace, is that asking too much?

First there must be color, which is the same
thing Henri thinks as he looks up and knows
he must paint Van Gogh's portrait, all the pain
there, the vast hunger, all the rage that shows
itself in planes and shapes that never rest,
that are in motion as he vows to paint
a portrait of his friend Toulouse-Lautrec.

Looking down, Vincent knows he has been seen.
All the folds of Henri's face disappear
and rosy petals blossom from his head,
so delicate in this light, so sheer.
Vincent smiles. Tanguy's shop is just ahead.

II

BITTERSWEET NIGHTSHADE

"Variable, and therefore, miserable condition of man! this minute I was well, and am ill, this minute. I am surprised with a sudden change, and alteration to worse."

—John Donne, *Devotions upon Emergent Occasions*

ONCOGENE

Before eyes, before eye color, before
fingers, before breath and cry, it was there.
Nothing to be seen or touched, something more
like a current, a stirring of the air.

When he stood by his desk in second grade
muttering through the pledge of allegiance,
it was there. At ten, the first time he played
cello solos before an audience,

it was there. A readiness in the cells,
an occult passion for growth. When he dreamed,
it was there as the secrets a ghost tells
while the wind shifts. In moonlight as it gleamed

through lids half-open in sleep, it was there.
It was there when he ran beside a creek
at first light, taking the sharp winter air
into the soft tissue of lungs grown weak

now, though he is only forty years old,
though he was strong, though it began somewhere
deep in his bones. That day when he was told,
he already knew. It was always there.

BRAIN LESIONS

"Memory is affected in specific ways by damage to different parts of the brain."
—Daniel L. Schacter, *Searching for Memory*

I.

She knows the face in the mirror
is a face but does not know it
is her own. This house she knows
to be a house, and it contains
the glass that contains both the face
that looks back at her and the man
poised beside the woman standing there.

His gnarled fingers are the same shape
as his lips and his gray hair is wild
from wind when they drove to this place
he calls her home. It is his voice
that tells her who he is, her Edward,
for how could a woman forget the man
she has loved since childhood?

He is moving aside as though pulled
by the hand that never found its way
into the glass. This dress he brought
for her to wear is so old and shapeless.

Now he returns from somewhere just beyond
the glass to produce a slim young woman
whose chin and mouth anyone can tell
are just like his. She settles between
them and stares with the same hazel
eyes as the woman they hold in place

with their gaze while bright light
pours through a window behind them.

II.

The man kneeling by the azaleas
thinks it is time for him to return
to barracks. First he wants to write
a quick letter to his girl up in Maine
who was sick with a cold the last time
he heard from her. When was that?
Late December, and here it is April
of 'forty-four. Worried that he will
never learn those semaphore signals,
that the war will end before he can
return to the front, that his Top
Sergeant drinks too much whiskey,
he rises and turns toward the open
door where his nurse Clyde bellows
about coming inside. Time for dinner
and the news. There are signs of life
on Mars, Clyde says, and President
Clinton is going to see his daughter
dance Swan Lake. Clyde says all
the rest are seated and hands him
a glass of water. He assumes Clyde
meant Harry Truman, though he is
certain Roosevelt is still in office.
About life on Mars he can only laugh.
Orson Welles tried that one back
in 'thirty-eight, just after the war began.
He sits down and takes off his hat,
which says "Los Angeles Dodgers"
and seems to be a terrible joke.
Brooklyn is his favorite team.

III.

The man who spent a lifetime
writing love songs loves to see
deer walk across the grass
in dawn light. Watching them
from bed, he thinks their legs
must feel glued to the ground
till the moment comes for running,
as though each step required
deep thought. In his brain now
there is nothing approaching
song. He admires the way
a doe's ears twitch in the wind
as she listens for danger,
the way she dips her chest
gracefully down toward the last
autumn flowers by the apiary

and brings Margaret running
from the house. His wife,
he remembers that. But nothing
about her or himself, nothing
of the songs she sings at night
while a fire crackles behind
them as she says it did when he
wrote them for her. He loves her
stories of their charmed life
together, a life full of color
photographs and record albums
that bring nothing back for him.
They lie scattered around him now,
stripped clear of visible life
like the flowerbeds these deer
leave behind as they flee.

IV.

She smiles at him and says she reads
all the time, simply all the time,
and they cannot get enough books
in the Home to satisfy her needs.
She writes, too, though not as much
nor as well as he does, and has
published a few poems over the years,
here and there, nowhere he would
have heard of. She turns away,
sees the piles of his books and picks
one up, flipping through the pages.

She turns back and her face ignites
with pleasure. She smiles and tells
him she reads all the time, simply
all the time. They cannot get enough
books in the Home to satisfy her needs.
She looks down at the book in her hand
and admits she writes a little herself,
a few poems now and again, published
over the years, nowhere he would
have heard about. She takes two steps
toward the row of seats, notices the book
in her hand, spins around and tells
him she reads all the time simply
all the time. She shows him what
is in her hand and says *See?*

BEDRIDDEN

Spring

Darkness lingered all morning
in treetops and the late sleep
of tulips. Fog linked me by faith
alone to hills across the valley.
Now sunlight begins to lift
night as a vapor from stone
and soil while faint breezes probe
the oak leaves. Only birdsong
is needed to grant this day
its place among the pantheon
of Mays I remember from long ago,
those years before the first signs
of illness brought me to this bed.

Summer

Late at night I hear
the animals come to drink
by glow of the Dying Grass Moon.
Deer come. I watch them
stutter-step among the pond
rocks and gladiolas blooming
wilder this year than ever.
Raccoons come, their young
stumbling on pots of herbs,
and somewhere in the valley
below a dog howls to still
the yearning in its heart.
Driven by thirst, stray cats
come, prowling the edge
of my yard, all eyes.

Twin oaks, their branches
curving themselves around
the light, call morning down.

Autumn

I wake to see a flock of red and gold
leaves come to rest on Russian sage
that August spread like a comforter
across my yard. Soon a gust stirs them,
though a few clutch the blue haze
of flowers still in bloom.
The light says early afternoon.
There seemed to be no time
between seasons, only ceaseless
heat leading straight to this
sudden cold. After a week
of rain, the clear sky
and sun made these leaves
sparkle in a soft breeze.

Winter

Winter mornings when the valley
is a river of mist, when I
can hear horses and cattle call
from everywhere at once and all
at once I see the river lift
itself to begin the slow drift
uphill toward me, there is no choice
but to close my eyes and give voice
to light that will soon be soaked in
mist the valley had been cloaked in.

BITTERSWEET NIGHTSHADE

It has been months since I could walk this far.
At noon the fence row thick with bittersweet
nightshade flashes with summer sun. There are
no clouds, no fleeing deer, no swirls of breeze,
nothing I remember from the last time
I was here. Now I prop my cane against
a post, lying back where the long stems climb
and scramble over everything that rests

in their way. I love to see these blue stars.
Their five points bend back to reveal a blunt
golden cone nestled in the heart of leaf
where in this light long shadows run like tears.
The wide yellow berries starting to run
toward red are the exact color of grief.

SELF-PORTRAIT WITH 1911 NY YANKEES CAP

The subtlest approach would be to ignore
the gray wool cap with its halo of air
vents, its navy blue button, monogram
and bill. The rounded, crownless fit and air
of slapdash speed should also be ignored
so that the grandeur of the monogram
can assert itself. Of course the Yankees
in 1911 were a weak team
best known for hitting triples and stealing
bases. They were a shadow of the teams
that later came to rule baseball, Yankee
teams who began their greatness by stealing
Babe Ruth from the Red Sox January
Third, 1920. Little Birdie Cree
was the kind of player who wore this cap.
Although a true wizard with the bat, Cree
kept getting hurt and in January
of 1916 relinquished his cap
and flannels for good to settle beside
the Susquehanna and work in machine
parts. Birdie was my size, too small to play
every day. The body is a machine
after all, and must fit its tasks. Besides,
Cree was temperamental, someone who played
hard, I imagine from his statistics,
and did not consider that his body
might give out. Medical science was far
behind where it is now, when the body
seems to yield its secrets and statistics
to tell us with grave certainty how far
we have let ourselves drift from perfect health.
Yet medical science cannot today
explain how a virus that found its way
to my brain six years ago can today

be responsible for my shattered health
or how my thoughts get lost along the way
whenever I deal with abstract ideas.
In the mirror, the old cap I forgot
I was wearing gives me a new idea
which, as I turn to note it, I forget.

AUTUMN EQUINOX

I feel my body letting go of light
drawn to the wisdom of a harvest moon.
I feel it welcome the lengthening night
like a lover in early afternoon.

My dreams are windfall in a field gone wild.
I gather them through the lengthening night
and when they have all been carefully piled
my body begins letting go of light.

Indian summer to leaf-fall to first frost
the memories that were carefully piled
become the dreams most likely to be lost.
My dreams are windfall in a field gone wild

now that memory has abandoned them,
now that Indian summer, leaf-fall, first frost
have become the same amazing autumn
skein of those dreams most likely to be lost.

I feel my body letting go of light.
I feel it welcome the lengthening night,
the windfall of dreams that have long been lost
to Indian summer, leaf-fall, and first frost.

A CHANGE OF WEATHER

Tonight I hear the rising autumn wind
and whirling leaves. I hear the heavy rain
arrive as if released from deep within
the wind like rage, or a sudden insane
blossoming of pain, the kind that woke me
in time to hear this headlong rush of rain.

Some nights I dream of health as a calm sea.
Some nights a clearing in an alpine wood
awash in meadowgrass. But it could be
a storm, a swirling tempest in the blood
like a cyclone sweeping everything clean,
leaving wreckage in its wake, death, a flood
of grief. That would be the place to begin.
Tonight I hear the rising autumn wind.

CHANNEL

In time the fork my life took
as illness changed its course
will wander to the main stream
and there below the long waterfalls
and cataracts I will begin my rush
to the place I was going from the start.
I imagine looking back to see
the silted mass where a huge bend
holds sunlight in a net of evergreen
and the sky unable to bear its own
violet brilliance a moment longer.
Out of shadows where the channel
crumbles comes the raucous sound
a great blue heron makes when startled.
Scent of peppermint rides breezes
from the valley and I catch hints
of current beneath the surface
just as darkness unfurls.
There I imagine what was lost
coming together with what was gained
to pour itself at last into the sea.

III

THE PROPER SEASON

CRITICAL CARE

Nothing

not the fall crop
of fat blackberries that dazzle
now where they have hidden all month
from daylong sun
in a quirk of gnarled scrub oak

nor the suddenly gold leaves
dropping
from maples as we cross the creek
bone dry since early June

nor twin fawns in their spots
still too innocent to run
from what danger we pose

prepares us
to come inside
and see you lying there
in a wash of brilliant light
breathing
only when an eggshell blue
bellows drives the air into you

HER GAME

The nightly round of gin
rummy and shot of schnapps.
They both play to win.
The TV, one of their props,
flickers unwatched, the tints
wrong, the sound low.

She is 88. He hints
her mind and wits are slow
now, no match for his. This
is false and he knows it. Another
prop, such banter; it's his
specialty. He calls her "mother"
when he is close to losing,
Rosie when winning. She'll shake
her head and say "choosing
you was a serious mistake."

The time he had fare
left for one only,
she said she did not care
to walk, rode the trolley
home herself, and made
him walk the mile through rain.

She underknocks. Played
perfectly. It's still her game.

MAX AT TABLE

Piecework at 83;
hats, a stole, maybe
a full coat at peak
season.
       He speaks
of strolls along the edges
of Central Park, dredges
up memories of the best
furs on the west
side.
       Rosie looks
hours for the smooth beets
he loves. She cooks
a pullet, braises
fennel in olive oil, then
slowly raises
her eyes in prayer
before she eats
facing him and the same square
of dark that's always been there
over his left shoulder.

He says she's getting older.
She says *amen*.

TOOMEY'S DINER

Sundays at dawn were whispers and silent
pissing on the inside of the privy bowl.
If belt buckles merely clicked, zippers
crept shut, and the heels of heavy shoes
only thudded together muffled in our hands,
mother slept on as we crept out the door.

Sunday mornings my face seemed to melt
in ripples of chrome circling high stools
at the bar of Toomey's Diner. The air
inside was thick with breath and smokes
as I spun between my father and brother
waiting for our *flapjacks all around*.
I saw the soles of my feet turned upside
down in the stools' silvery pedestals
and knew enough to spin without a squeak.

So this was the world outside. Red leather
to sit on, red Formica edged in chrome
where my elbows fit, red menus studded
with paper clips. Signs said Special Today.
This was the stuff of weekday dreams. A small
jukebox at every table, rice to keep
the salt dry, toothpicks, a great pyramid
of cereal boxes hiding the cook.
Sunday was sizzling grease and apple juice
glowing pink, then blue in the sudden shift
of neon. Sunday laughter gave off such
heat that walls burst with sweat.

When the day came apart, I always had
the relative silence of knives and forks
on plates, the delicate lids of syrup holders
snapping shut, coffee slurped from steaming mugs,
coins on the counter, the sound of our bill
skewered by Toomey as we turned to leave.

VISITING HOUR

We came straight from school,
crossing the island as winds
rose and fell. From half
a mile away the whitecapped
baywater smelled of fuel oil,
marsh grass, and autumn
darkness. Gulls circled
a trawler nudging the dock.
We gathered in an alley
behind the old hospital
where our fathers recovered,
or declined, or lingered
behind the cold panes keeping
them from us. We were too young
and full of dangerous life
to be allowed inside. Stroke,
cancer of the lung, a broken
hip, severed arm, failing heart.
We named our fathers by what held
them there. Clot, stone, spine.
Taking turns to stand on one
another's shoulders, we tapped
on windows as the sun set.
Fathers smiled within the folds
of their faces, waved, lay back
among the pillows. They turned
white before our eyes, became
empty spaces in our lives,
quiet behind glass in their
gleaming ground floor rooms.

TERMINAL

My father is coming home on this train.
Its headlight shatters the October rain
as it rocks across a narrow trestle
onto the island and blasts its whistle.
The dripping engine curves toward the station
with a hiss spread before it like a stain.

The past is no longer his dark domain.
I wander among the ghostly people
       my father is coming home
with, hoping he will know me with this cane
in my hand, know I have chosen the same
gnarled wood as his own two canes, light hazel
from southern Italy, with the curved handle
worn smooth. I can see him through the cracked pane.

LEAKAGE

Sight bleeds away deep within my mother's eyes.
Haze for years clouded the world as she knew it,
then holes slowly filled the center of her vision
field till all she saw was a circle of indigo
and sharp shadows in azure on the periphery.
Her eyes bulged as though in shock at what could
be lost to scarring and the steady leakage of fluid.
When I look at the gleaming dark center, it gives back
a light she no longer recognizes. Yet her gaze
turns only outward, fierce as ever in its search
of the one place there is no hope of clear sight.

MEMORY HARBOR

*"No one creates. The artist assembles
memories."*
                              —*Jack B. Yeats*

I no longer know what to trust
when the past comes into view
like a harbor and the boat
my father pilots begins to swing
in one great arc toward the sea.
His face catches the grim morning
light and my mother in the window
of a shack turns away from the view,
fading into the dark. But my father
was a poultry butcher in the city
and my mother never rose with morning
light in their whole life together.

Didn't we live by the sea at the end
and didn't we turn away from one another
morning and night? Wasn't our home
the heart of storm, our shore given
over to the wrack of ebb and flow?

I no longer know where to turn
when loss like a gust of wind
swings me back again to open sea
where the sun that I knew as a smooth
disk rising behind me grows edges
now as it sets and glows coral
and bittersweet, glows crimson
and scarlet in the moment it sinks
below the shimmering horizon.

EVENING SONG

A flare of daylight sets my face ablaze
in its frame above her bed as the sun
sinks. Full Indian summer but these days
she is always cold, always wanting one

more layer of clothes or cup of hot tea,
grumbling as she hugs herself and paces.
She feels dark vapors in the air, traces
of dust. This is not where she wants to be.

When she sits, a shard of memory glows
and fades, the past an empty theater gone
dark the moment she arrives, curtain closed,
orchestra never launching into song.

For years she has been slowly going blind,
drawing the world into her corner room
beside the sea, drenched in endless gloom.
I am no longer in my mother's mind.

END STAGE

My brother rises from his easy chair,
staggering as the darkness follows him.
The soles of his feet feel nothing at all
but he has learned how to embrace the air
and sway across the rhythm of his heart.

As his movements loosen, time falls apart
till he finds himself braced against the wall.
His steps have shrunken with his sight and there
is little he can follow beyond the dim
edge of hope that leads him down the hall.

His barefoot shuffling is the sound an old
man makes but he will never get that far.
Now he would settle for the bedroom door
and a slight breeze from the open window
that tells him where he is and nothing more.

He enters a shaft of light and turns gold
for a moment, his skin glowing as though
radiant with warmth. Yet he is always cold,
growing paler as the day wanes, and light
no longer makes a difference. At night

when childhood is the center of his life,
memories and dreams are the only sight
he has. There is something he wants to know,
he says, something important that we are
missing. I listen, knowing he is right.

THE BREAKERS

At last Kate Stone had her view of the sea.
After nearly seventy years with Jack
in blaring and sooty New York City,
harsh decades of apartments atop fur
shops, they had come to water. Kate sat back,
adjusting the wool blankets across her
lap, and leaned her head against a red brick
wall. She breathed in salt air, feeling the way
crystals had settled in folds of her neck
already and built up under her gray

eyes like a residue of tears. The sea.
She could even hear it. That is, if Jack
would ever shut up, she could. A city
street all by himself! Look at him: that fur
hat he made, black to match his hair, his back
still straight, his hand reaching over to her,
his face in the wind as red as the brick
of this wall. Jack Stone. Kate still loved the way
saying his name to herself made her neck
tingle all the way up into the gray

hair, thinning now, that crowned her head that held
the growth that meant they could come to the sea
at last. Kate closed her eyes and sighed. She smelled
fish, she was sure of it. An odor from
childhood, the market in Gdansk where she
loved to see the vacant eyes of fish come
alive as she passed, though her mother said
it was a cloud moving across the sun
and nothing more. A shadow. What was dead
was dead. But Kate knew better. If someone

looked long and hard, she would see what was held
in the eye of a fish fresh from the sea,

a secret kept by ice, a secret that smelled
the way a man smelled when he came home from
the docks at night. Kate looked up. What was she
thinking about! Such craziness would come
to her out of nowhere. The doctor said
it was the disease. Stay out of the sun,
since it hurt her eyes. Might as well be dead
already. Grains, cooked greens, meat only one

meal a day and not red either. Fruit was
fine, but she was not dying in a good
season for fruit, which was just her luck. Does
anyone die in the proper season?
Mama and Papa both in spring. Kate could
be gone by late spring too. But the reason
she knew she must live through the year was Jack,
sick with the failing heart. He would surely
die if she went first, since the next attack,
that German cardiologist said, would be

his last. She loathed that Doctor Frisch, who was
aloof and harsh at the same time. A good
heart man, everyone told them, but what does
that matter in a heart's final season?
Kate would accept no dying while Jack could
still breathe. They were one another's reason
to live! Had been since the scorching day Jack
had sashayed into Papa's store—surely
sent by God himself—and seemed to attack
his cream soda like a man who might be

dead in two more seconds from thirst. *Jack Stone*,
he said, *from Danzig*. Papa dropped a glass.
He stood looking down, trying to compose
himself, then studied the man gulping cream
soda at his fountain, took in the mass
of curling hair, dark eyes, the nose that seemed

broken six ways down its length, the full lips,
and risked it: *perhaps you said Gdansk?* That
was all it took. Jack had grown up just steps
from the Vistula and had known her fat

Aunt Anna, her Uncle Cass. Mama Stone,
killed by Nazis, came from Austrian glass
makers. Papa Stone was a composer
at heart, a stevedore by trade. With skin like cream,
soft hands, an eye for furs, Jack would amass
a fortune, he claimed. Destiny. It seemed
that all he needed, as Kate watched his lips
form the words, was a wife to help him, that
he was prepared then to take any steps
needed to win her Papa over. *Fat*

chance, Kate said when she heard. Who knows, maybe
it was his persistence, visits five nights
a week, always flowers in his hand, three
yellow roses. Maybe the sleek fox stole
he made for her, or his smile. By all rights
she should have married the young dentist, Joel
Schatz, by now a millionaire, or the tall
diamond merchant with his blue eyes and gray
hair even at twenty-two, Louis Small
his name was, a real gem. Ha! She would say,

though not to Jack's face, that she was maybe
a blessed woman after all. From those nights
in that place to these nights here in just three
winks of the eye! Suddenly they were old.
The sea was speaking with the voice of light.
Suddenly there were all these gaping holes
where her memories once were. Jack was tall
in the wintry sun before her eyes, gray
skin crinkling as he smiled down at her small
form tilted back in the wheelchair, and said

Wake up, Katie, it's time to have a look
at the breakers. And she knew that was all
she had wanted, to place her foot beside
his in the sea at last. So what if fall
was in the air, or if they caught a chill
and died? No one cared if the ebbing tide
swept them away. So this is how we will
do it, she thought. At first, they will hold one
another up as they move through the sand.
He will kneel to take off her shoes. The fun
will start when she does the same for him and

he sees she can stand on her own. That look
will be something to treasure. Because all
she needed was for him to stand beside
her. Then they can turn to watch the waves fall
all over themselves, they can take the chill
air deep into their lungs and laugh the tired
laughter of all those missing nights that will
suddenly be back before them. In one
instant, their toes sinking into the sand,
his eyes finding the moon and hers the sun,
their bodies will rise into the sky and

they will feel the past wash over them again,
everything all at once like the beauty
of three yellow roses, or like the sea
in the moment the tide stops coming in.

IV

PURE GIFT

"Water is beginning, is end, is pure, is pure gift."
—Louise MacNeice, *"Our Sister Water"*

RIVER WALK

Two gray sculls glide through morning river mist,
sunlight dazzling their gunwales, oars winking
white at their dripping tips. I am thinking
of you while I watch them move as though kissed

by grace. You are on midwest waters now,
canoeing lakes where winter comes early.
Alone, I see in your hand the pearly
nautilus, hear you explain to me how

it lived and died. I feel your skin on mine,
your body instead of my cane beside
me for balance. I can smell the flood tide
again and you, tasting slightly of brine,

are so present here that I no longer
feel your loss, at least not until I turn
east to face the rising sun that will burn
off the mist. Then the light will grow stronger,

I will see that these sculls crease the surface,
not float on mist, and will tell myself you
and I are apart, as we always knew
we had to be. It is not much solace

to have known ahead of time what time would
do. We took our time. We moved as these teams
of scullers do, through a fusion of dreams,
our bodies in unison, and withstood

the current as best we could. The surprise
is not this pain I feel, but my pleasure
while I watch your paddle dip and feather
the water clearing right before my eyes.

THE WINTER BRANCH

"All pleasures and all pains, remembering
The bough of summer and the winter branch."
            —Wallace Stevens, "Sunday Morning"

Spare me metaphor on Sunday mornings
in February. News of the pell-mell
downhill skier ramming a snow-making
machine in France drives me outside
for a slow walk along the river.
A tug's wake rocks the mustard-hulled
sailboat docked alone in winter moorage.
A log broken from its raft and twisting
downriver is home to a squawking mallard
drake. A voiceless spaniel I see daily
yaps at me when I pass him on the bank.

All I want are facts. This is my one
thousand one hundred seventy third day
of being sick. My temperature seldom
rises above 97 and the fluid in my spine's
fouled canal teems with excess protein.
The world I walk in tilts to the left.
Because my slow wave sleep is nothing
but a fragmented vase, dreams it might
hold are lost. I awaken in a wash
of moonlight as the night breeze turns.
Holes formed in my brain draw random
bits of the past into themselves
and sometimes consume the present
before I can find a place to store it.
If we were to meet now, if I were
to look at you closely while you spoke,
I am likely to forget your name.

Stopping above a cove where steelhead feed,
where the river bends and a concrete ramp
has sunk into silt, I understand it is time
to lay my cane aside and sit and stare,
drawn at last far enough outside myself
to see what is really there. Behind me,
I saw in the window of a riverfront condo
an elderly couple side-by-side on their couch,
backs to the view, using the morning light
to read the same news I had read. Before me,
eight oars in unison stroke and feather
as a crew pulls south. Wind-borne laughter
reaches me like mist a quarter mile away,
just as two wet-suited men on jet sleds
roar past them to loop each other's wakes.
Their noise is the current given voice
and its rage takes my breath away.
So slowly I do not notice it till the sky
is fully gray, the morning's mild weather
has relapsed to rain. Rapt by the warm
front moving toward the Cascade foothills,
I had just begun noticing all the trees
on Ross Island are evergreen. Somewhere
in their tops, I know great blue heron nest.

HURRICANE WATCH

Another tropical
storm picking up speed in the Caribbean
becomes a hurricane
aiming for the barrier island
where my mother
still lives.

Again
she refuses to move from its path,
claiming herself
far above
danger in her fourth story
beachfront apartment.

No X taped
across her windows like a target,
no furniture shifted
away from the windowside,
nothing
to let the storm
or whatever is behind it
think for one moment
the woman can be threatened.

Hanging up
the phone
a continent away from her,
I am
back on the beach in the eye
of a hurricane.
I am
ten years old and alone
in the calm's
eerie light

breathing in the charged air,
              waiting
       for the next inevitable
furious blast to arrive.

NEAR THE END

My mother came to live beside the sea.
She hated the sound of surf, smell of brine,
gulls circling before the window where she
sat all day in a bright rage of sunshine.

Everyone was old. Everyone was slow.
They went to sleep too soon, rose too early,
were content to watch films and play bingo,
chat with staff and kowtow to the surly
young women at the front desk. Everyone
had someone living close enough to come
for visits twice a week. One woman's son
tried to move in though he was much too young.

There was something wrong with the moon and sun.
Her worst time was near the end of each day.
The moon rose, the sun set. She was alone
with darkness, chill, and fog over the bay.

SLIEVEMORE

—Achill Island, Ireland

This is where the sea of my childhood ends,
a cone of quartz and mica where sheep graze
above the golden curve of Dugort Strand
and tombs that date to the New Stone Age.

This is what I was looking towards those nights
I left the shouting behind to stand where
surf drew back into itself and streetlights
from home grew dimmer in the salty air.

In the galaxy of the wave I could
travel to the ocean's outer reaches
with one deep breath. In a raft of driftwood
I could land on the deserted beaches

of villages cloaked in mist. They all looked
like this. Small white houses to welcome me
under weathered crags like Slievemore, fleece hooked
on gorse, moorgrass swaying, and a calm sea.

HOP FIELDS IN WINTER

By midsummer, twining hop vines will hide
these wires in a mob of bracts and flowers
that seem to mass in a matter of hours,
filling the dense air with a scent of pine.
But now, strung like harps, the fields sing in winds
raging downvalley. We watch as they pass
over the skin of the swollen river
and leave the impression that nothing lasts.

Brackish water ripples over the banks.
Wind tears into a stand of second growth
oak. In a moment, snow begins, thick flakes
in their smooth quadrille reminding us both
of cherry blossoms in late April let
loose in one great squall. I believe you are
thinking of spring planting as you look west
where the road bends and see the Coast Range clear.

We can feel the air warming. Where the storm
has been, morning light drenches the snowpack
before creeping toward us, nudging the dark
away. The wires wink, shiver, but hold firm.

DAY OF THE RAINBOW

"Until everything was rainbow, rainbow, rainbow!"
—Elizabeth Bishop, "The Fish"

The day we drove straight into a rainbow
began with ocean wind and spindrift gone
wild inside Whale Cove. We saw spume glow
as though praising the memory of dawn
and waves charge the early morning air
like a storm front. Across an arc of beach
a couple walked the dark parabola where
bare trunks lay tangled beyond the tide's reach.

We saw swash drench salt-fretted sandstone
till the cliff seemed to shudder, though we knew
it was only wind stroking the grassy backbone
of Depoe Bay. Since there was a shaft of blue
sky like a quill in clouds above the headland,
and light was strong enough to hint those clouds
lacked passion for a storm, we went to stand
where the downwarped land had long ago drowned

a river that once had emptied here.
Above us two herring gulls wheeled back
and began their swoop to scavenge the shore,
heads dusky for winter, white wings tipped black,
bills agape as they rose squealing and still
hungry from the breakers. Even as the sky
absorbed them in its own granite will
we knew it was another trick of the eye—

if we held our place they would reappear
against the surf in a flash of underbelly.
But more than anything, it was the sheer
force of the gulls' appetite that made us see

the time had come to start our journey home.
From Otis to the Coast Range the Salmon River,
gorged with snowmelt, its center all foam
and silt, raised its voice as though to deliver

a curse on the new year. We guessed we were
mastering the signs since the day we drove
straight into a rainbow the rain itself never
found us. Soon we passed a hazelnut grove
near Grand Ronde and the sky before us burst
into brilliance! The fallow valley would
have been enough to show nothing was cursed,
not when sodden wheat and onion fields could

suddenly imply a dazzle of July
in green and gold at the edge of the eye.
But we had more. We saw a rainbow span
the road. We saw that one end began
in an orchard north of Highway 99,
rising from a cluster of grape vines
like the essence of scent made visible,
and the other began in the hill

that kept our home hidden among scrub oak,
maple and Douglas fir. Despite the cloak
of clouds that blocked the sun, we saw above
us true color could hold fast as we drove,
could endure and even lead us to our door.
I thought backwards one hour to the shore
surely buried now by storm surge and tide.
I thought ahead, then put my thoughts aside.

PROTECTION ISLAND

We lie rocking leeward of Protection
Island, knowing the silence of the sea
is a promise a night at sea will break.
Even daylight is raucous as we climb
on deck to view an early spring sunrise—
and a young bald eagle lift from the scree
with a Bonaparte gull in its talons
trailing the gull's mate shrieking in its wake.
This island is a bird sanctuary;
all around us the air is filled with cries
as gulls scatter and return one more time.
Without my cane I lean against my wife
to watch them shift and settle in the light.
I cannot keep my balance on the sea.

SWANS IN GALWAY BAY

Seven pairs of swans preen
this morning near the docks.
We walk down together
searching among the rocks
for a perfect feather
to commemorate the scene.

The swans float, one foot still
tucked underneath a wing,
the other held steady
as a rudder. They seem
both unconcerned and ready
for whatever the day will

bring them as they drift past.
Soon they are swept away
in pairs where the River
Corrib surges into Galway Bay—
from here just a sliver
of jagged slate-blue glass

but fierce enough to spin
them sideways toward the sea.
Paired still, they carry on
their slow ceremonies,
adjusting with utter calm
to the currents they move in,

content, it would appear,
to end up wherever
they find themselves as long
as they are together,
each feather where it belongs,
each mate with a clear

line of sight to the other.
We have come to the docks'
end emptyhanded. I turn
back, but she stops to watch,
holding me there as one
small feather drifts to shore.

V

DAYBREAK

SEDUCTION

A cerise robe crumpled
on her ash duvet, a vase
of crimson columbine, grapes
in glazed bowls on the window
ledge. Wicker shadows
mottle the scatter rug
where his clothes were tossed.

Ivory skies at dusk
are rinsed coral by sheer
curtains streaming with summer
wind. Their gazes go
separate ways, his
to the trellis of cobwebs
like smoke above the bed,
hers to the bright red
rose in a poster on the wall,
then slowly turn inward.

One thing led to the next,
light across her flushed throat,
an arm tangled in bedsheets
as it hung just above
the floor, her eyes grown
hazy as they found him.
Rooms opened into other rooms,
two pasts becoming the only
possible present, a sudden
complement of colors seeming
too far apart to bring
this much to life.

STILL LIFE WITH EGGS & WHISK

Eggs on a white background, eggs in a glass
bowl, and a whisk twined in its own shadow.
She works with shade and light, getting the mass
and depth right, bringing the late morning glow
that warms our house on clear November days
down to drench the delicate surfaces
of these half dozen eggs that hold her gaze.

They turn the yellow of ground irises
where warmth within them rises to the shell
and now it is time for the air around
them to seep lavender. Soon I can smell
it, the pungent herb of love, and the sound
filling the room as she paints is the same
sound hearts might make when they burst into flame.

SOURWOOD NOCTURNE

August nights the sourwood droops
with creamy white flowers that come
and go as though the dark of fall

were pure illusion. Walking some
nights on a deer trail that loops
the hillside, we can believe all

we hope for is present in one
deep breath. Then a moment
later is September. The slight

sourwood leaves turn such brilliant
scarlet it seems summer sun
still smolders in the tree's heart.

This high the evening light runs
toward December in a large wash
of blues, translucent as time

tightens and the air grows harsh.
Something moves behind us, a summons
within the wind. We turn toward home.

DAYBREAK

The shapes that moved outside
our door tonight were four deer
come to feed on the last winter
weeds. The riot of their flight
seemed to echo through the dark
when I left my bed to see them.

Now the valley sends its voices
up through morning mist. Cows low,
the sheep farmer's old border
collie barks as she herds strays
and the southbound freight is
an hour late. Where our hillside
plummets, a fringe of feathery
wild grasses webbed with frost
bends as though lost in prayer.

My wife built this house round
because a clear loop of moonlight
found the space for her early
on a morning like this. She woke
in her down sleeping bag under
a canopy of second growth to hear
great horned owls call from oaks
creaking in a sudden surge of wind.
When she sat up, there was a deer
standing exactly where a dowser
had told her the well should go.

CASSEROLE

One cutting board is maple,
the other oak. One knife is
serrated, its blade afloat
in a black plastic handle,
the other honed keen tonight
in a flourish of cross-strokes
against the sharpening steel.
My wife stands beside me,
purple and yellow pepper
slices heaped where she has
tossed them among the lemon
wedges, halved red onions,
and wafers of garlic.

I have cut three summer squash
in quarter-inch disks that match
rounds of Japanese eggplant
and Roma tomatoes stacked
like sentinels by the oiled
pan as our oven heats.
She lifts a handful of eggplant
to spread across the bottom
of the dish, topping it
with tomatoes for their moisture.
I distribute the garlic,
red onion and lemon in
spaces she leaves clear for me.
We take turns draping lacy
pepper ribbons over squash
she scattered on the layers
and soon the fragrance of deep
summer is swirling round us.

I pause to watch her fingers
strip thyme from its stem and crush

the oval leaves. She reaches
past me for sweet marjoram
I diced and piled with my blade.
In the moment our fingers
touch, I begin to sense how
this will all come together
under a cover of foil,
separate flavors merging
as it steeps in its juices.

FROGS RETURNING MOON

The creek is running wild with April rain
this morning. It tumbles down the hillside
and rushes under our bedroom windows,
humbling the dark-eyed junco's rolling trill.
Bees work the hyssop at our window sill,
its scent mixed with the rosemary and chives.
A Wilson's warbler flashes past, belly
like a glimpse of sun. Here and there a few
late daffodils and irises remain,
and the last lilacs are lavender-blue,
but all around a bold palette of new
life is taking over their fading lights.

It is not enough to sit in bed, rapt
but apart; after a six-month relapse
I am ready for a long walk outside.
The Douglas fir is tipped with pale green shoots
and even last year's failed azalea thrives.
Soon there will be marigolds and cosmos
in bloom, bleeding heart, a spread of seathrift,
and down the slope a shock of wild wood rose.
It is the month of Frogs Returning Moon,
spider eggs in gaps between steps, a nest
of mice in oak logs. Nothing is at rest.
The coyotes' howl fills the dwindling nights.

THE GEM

The girdle of an opal
in my wife's hand
gives off pale blue
and milky white fire
in the moonlight.

Her thumb strokes
the stone's sharp pavilion,
the crown, the star
and bezel facets
as though soaking
up their brilliance.

Across her body
day takes the shape
of swirling wind
and fast moving cloud.

A lemon yellow tulip
drenched with dew
outside our window,
drooping purple irises,
lilacs and late daffodils—

everything she has
nurtured for years
now seems ready to burst
with the fire in her hand.

FLIGHT

The summer night is flying
by, rattling windows where light
is alive. Bats are shadows,
brilliant flickers in a mist
of insects, and bumblebees
circle the hyssop. The air
thickens. Directly above
us now a small plane crosses
the horizon of the half
moon on its way to the sea.

This is a night even deer
might soar. We believe they are
searching for a wind somewhere
within the thicket of wild
rose, hazel and blackberries.
We believe the dark whisper
of grasses to be an owl's
wing prints, the drift of oak leaves
an echo of shifting tides
from beyond the Coastal Range.

As silence glides in gentle
spirals back to the earth, first
the sheen, then the shock of all
we have seen comes clear. This is
the moment we know pure flight
has little to do with lift
or drag and much to do with
dreams. It is the moment we
turn together to begin
our own powerful ascent.